Perception & My Revelation of the 23rd Psalm

GRACE MICHAELS

GRACE MICHAELS

PERCEPTION

Preface

I felt well compelled to sit down and write this book to help those struggling to find purpose and inspiration in our challenging world conditions. Especially the many people under Covid-19 lock-down who have not been able to meet their friends or families! And many others facing financial or health problems – as highlighted almost daily in world news and social media platforms.

I have personally learnt to look away from the troubles around me and to look to God for relief and release, I have studied the Bible and the writings of Mary Baker Eddy for more than 20 years and know that this is the truth; and I have been able to demonstrate and outwork this truth in my own life. I feel compelled to share it with everyone – particularly in these times of need.

No matter what devastation surrounds the human being, it's not the ultimate reality, it's not the absolute law and it's not forever 'fixed'. There is a superior law that operates uninterruptedly – and that gives transcendent power to those who operationalise it.

There is a great need for humanity to change the way we think!

Baker Eddy.

My references are directly quoted from the Bible, Science and Health with Key to the Scriptures by Mary Baker Eddy and also Miscellaneous Writings, also by Mary Baker Eddy

I have also included notes from various Christian Scientists whose writings have inspired me over the years.

I hope this very concise book helps you to start your journey in finding the truth, or even if you are already familiar with it, inspires you to explore it more deeply. I hope you enjoy reading this book.

Copyright: Grace Michaels

Table of Contents

Perception

What we see through our physical senses is restrictive and flawed and does not reveal the true nature of everything. It is only a hint of the perfection, reality and grandeur of spiritually real phenomena which fill all space.

What is it that imposes a perception - not the reality on each and everyone of us – it is the human mind. This baser mentality is in enmity with the Mind which is God. This mentality seems to find expression in a material man and a material universe, where as Mind in its full signification, finds expression in a spiritual man and a spiritual universe. Jesus pronounced this so-called mind a lie and the father of lies. Paul called it the carnal mind. Paul went on to say this mind has to be renewed, transformed and finally put off by everyone because this fleshly mind wars against the Spirit/ God.

The carnal mind, mortal mind or fleshly mind perceives everything in terms of limits. The imprisoning notions it imposes on us appear as our thoughts and become our experience. It is deceiving and wants us to identify thought and experience as two different things and yet it is the one thing – the lie. Perception is the problem.

" Erring human mind forces can work only evil under whatever name or pretence they are employed; for Spirit and matter, good and evil, light and darkness, cannot mingle". (Science & Health 186:7-10)

Our problems may vary from feeling imprisoned in our own bodies, failing relationships, governmental decisions we don't approve of, fluctuating economies, environmental conditions and diseases, because we rely on flawed perceptions imposed by the carnal mind.

These limits put upon us; our divine source, creator, could never know about, neither would He include them as part of His creation. He made us in His image and likeness and pronounced good to all that He made. He also gave man dominion over everything!

Mathew 4: 17
"... Jesus began to preach and to say, Repent: for the kingdom of heaven is at hand."

Repent refers to change of thinking, change the way you think, don't be fooled by mortal mind.

Spirit perception corrects the flawed misconceptions of the mortal mind we have been holding onto which are world-imposed.

There remains in everyone, the necessity for a more tangible concept, a more definite definition of Deity to meet practical needs of humanity. Moses, encouraging his followers in the wilderness, reminded them that God is Life. Paul refers to God as Mind in writing to the Philippians, he admonishes them to have the mind that was also in Christ Jesus. Jesus finding the Samaritan woman at the well said " God is Spirit; and they that worship Him must worship Him in spirit and truth. John the Apostle said " God is love; and he that dwelleth in Love, dwelleth in God, and God in Him"

God as Spirit is everywhere and all presence and all-knowing therefore, He is Mind and Mind cannot be disassociated from Life and Love.

But mind, life and love as humanly manifested are lamentably imperfect; only Love as unselfish, Mind unerring and Life above disease can they properly be held to be

Deity. To be said simply- only as they are sustained, vitalised, and impelled by Principle are they worthy names for God. And only as Principle is not abstract and mindless but imbued with Life, Mind, and Love, is it entitled to be as Deity. Then they are all transferred from the realm of the human to the divine. We can name Deity the following names: God/Love/Mind/Principle/Truth/Life/Soul/ Spirit.

The real spiritual man of God's creating as in **Genesis 1** is not the mortal man that is deceived by the mortal mind. This man is pure, perfect, complete and whole. He is innocent and remains untouched by human circumstances and remains inseparable from God.

One may ask "if this is true, in the absolute, that God is Mind and man is spiritual and perfect- but what has that to do with my present predicament or suffering, the seeming material condition and its distresses?"

The answer is: Instead of dwelling upon your aches and pains, try to dismiss them from thought; for they are not your thoughts; they are only false suggestions springing from mortal mind as explained above. Then direct attention, as best you can to the sublime truth that Life – your life is God, and that since God is everywhere and always expressing Himself perfectly, Life is everywhere and always functioning harmoniously and uninterruptedly even where the distress seems to be. The result as you hold steadfastly to the truth will be a change in consciousness, whereby your sense of sickness, which is false, gives place to the sense of health, which is true.

In cases of worry, confusion, mental impairment, personal or business problems that defy solution – there is no remedy so near, none so effective as to calmly insist that the all-knowing Mind, which is God, is never weary, never disturbed, never inadequate and that this Mind expresses itself and guides you in every right effort and undertaking.

You will find your thought clarifying and expanding. You will also find that while yourself could do nothing, you can with the genuine intelligence operating through you, cope successfully with the difficulties at hand.

"Hold thought steadfastly to the enduring, the good, and the true, and you will bring these into your experience proportionably to their occupancy of your thought." (Science & Health 261:4)

James 3: 17

The wisdom that is from above is first pure, then peaceable, gentle, and easy to be entreated, full of mercy and good fruits, without partiality, and without hypocrisy.

Luke 10: 19

Behold, I give you power to tread on serpents and scorpions, and over all the power of the enemy: and nothing shall by any means hurt you.

It is empowering to know that God's love does not condemn but it redeems and restores. Man as a child of God is pure and has no knowledge of sin. This goes further to state that no part of the real man has ever been injured, damaged or diseased as God is the Life of man and man is the idea of God. Nothing can enter the Mind which is God; to touch, disturb or threaten His beloved child.

This Truth knows no race, religion or creed neither does it discriminate on age, animal, blade of grass or a bird; therefore can be applied or sanctioned by anyone, and anywhere in this universe.

The Lord is my shepherd I shall not want

"All our dreams of life in matter can never in reality change the fact that our life is Spirit and our body harmonious and beautiful". (M.B.E Collection).

The spiritual view of Being is in divine reflection.

Isaiah 2: 22

Cease ye from man, whose breath is in his nostrils: for wherein is he to be accounted of?

John 6: 63

It is the Spirit that quickeneth; the flesh profiteth nothing.

Job 32: 8

There is a spirit in man: and the inspiration of the Almighty giveth them understanding.

The First book of Genesis in the Bible tells us man is created in God's image and likeness. Christ Jesus said in the Gospel of **John 5: 17**

"My Father worketh hitherto, and I work", this shows us that as God's children our work is simply reflection, we have "done- for- you" qualities which we simply reflect.

Our job or work is to realise this and recognise God's power and presence and His role as our father/Mother God taking care of His beloved creation.

God as our Father/Mother does not give us problems but simply goodness which is spiritual, perpetual, unchanging and unaffected by materiality. God as Love allows no fear, discouragement neither can He fall victim to world materialism.

Our God is omnipotent, omnipresent and omniscient- meaning He is all presence, all power and all science. There is no power against God. We have to view from this standpoint that our God is All -in all. Hear this declaration from God in Isaiah 40: 28 to 29 "Hast thou not known? Hast thou not heard, that the everlasting God, the Lord, the creator of the ends of earth, fainteth not, neither is weary? There is no searching for his understanding. He giveth power to the faint; and to those who have no might he increaseth strength".

God is always preserving man's spiritual identity, and we can look to this truth to correct any false picture suggesting otherwise. The understanding that man is governed only by God, good, removes the imposition another's actions might seem to place on us. We see the wrong action as simply a dream of mortal mind, and not representing someone's actual identity. The divine Mind is constantly imparting what is good, pure, and true about each individual. As we acknowledge this spiritual fact, we see a child of God in place of a thief, and another child of God in place of a victim. It's definitely a choice we're making, so let's choose wisely! " The kingdom of God is within you" **Luke 17: 21.** This does not mean the infinite, God is contained in the finite, for that would be impossible. Rather, infinite Spirit, God is reflected by man, and reigns within us. And if the kingdom of heaven is within me and everyone else, that is a consciousness of goodness, purity, health and holiness then there is no room for anything else in our thinking, and our bodies and environment reflect or manifest what is in thought.

Infinite Life which man expresses as God's reflection is independent of inert, mindless matter. We are not the medium of evil, disease, lack, poverty and any other horrible thing, but reflect and express God's goodness and harmony.

Man is held in one eternal round of harmonious being. What our heavenly Father knows about His children is only uninterrupted continuity of good.

The manifestation of Life and plenty in the real man is uninterrupted by the mesmerism of sickness, death, hard times, governmental upheavals, failing crops or business. His advancement and unfoldment are unimpeded by stagnation or reversal. His purity is uninterrupted by materiality; his intelligence is uninterrupted by stupidity and doubt, and his confidence is uninterrupted by fear. No hate, willfulness, selfishness, or other sin can halt the eternal continuity of man's consciousness of good and his character as the holy child of God. Let us know this and act accordingly.

All problems we experience in this world arise from suggestions of lack, inadequacy, depravity, insufficiency etc. These are only suggestions, and we should refute the lies and cleave unto our God.

Isaiah 54: 4, 5

4- Fear not; for thou shalt not be ashamed: neither be thou confounded; for thou shalt not be put to shame: for thou shalt forget the shame of thy youth, and shalt not remember the reproach of thy widowhood anymore.

5- For thy Maker is thine husband; the Lord of hosts is his name; and thy redeemer the Holy One of Israel; the god of the whole earth shall he be called.

We are truly never in want and are throughly furnished unto all good things by our Father/Mother God as His reflection. That includes health, wealth and well-being. The parable Jesus gave in the Bible of one lost sheep which a shepherd left the 99, to go and find the one, and after finding it celebrated with his neighbours to show his gratitude, shows clearly how much God cares for all of us.

He maketh me to lie down in green pastures

The great fact for all-time and eternity is that
God is All in all. He is the only creator, presence,
power, cause and effect. The next basic fact is
that man is created in God's likeness. This
means man is the effect of perfect cause and
so must exist at the standpoint of perfection.

This spiritual status of man is unassailable and
unalterable. He knows no bonds or limitations
because God has none. He needs nothing
because he already possesses all good. Man is
God's satisfied idea. Realising the all- presence
of God puts us in that safe spiritual existence
which is narrated in the first book of Genesis
as His image and likeness. This image and
likeness of God is actually-God manifested as
us. This idea of us as the reflection is never and
can never be separated from God Himself,
which means we are forever safe, untouched
by human circumstances and preserved by
our dear Father/Mother God.
 Here we are not viewing ourselves as a pitiful
mortal, but as a dearly loved child of God,
spiritual and perfect.

Luke 12: 32

Fear not, little flock; for it is your Father's good pleasure to give you the kingdom.

Philippians 4: 19

God shall supply all your need according to his riches in glory by Christ Jesus.

1 Thessalonians 5: 18

In everything give thanks: for this is the will of God in Christ Jesus concerning you.

Isaiah 45: 5, 6

5- I am the Lord, and there is none else, there is no God beside me: I girded thee, though thou hast not known me.

6- that they may know from the rising of the sun, and from the west, there is none beside me. I am the Lord and there is none else.

Man has no material history: God does not know it; therefore right now we can change our thought and pray to God to know Him better. No worries about the past that we cannot undo or the future, but the now is where we live and is what is important. Right now we are in the presence of all good.

He Leadeth me Besides the still waters

Hymn 354

1- Tis God the Spirit leads in paths before
unknown; the work to be performed is
ours, The strength is all His own.
2- Supported by His grace, we still pursue our
way; Assured that we shall reach the prize,
Secure in endless day.
3- God works in us to will, He works in us to
do; His is the power by which we act, His
be the glory too.

A solution to problems is always found in
faithfully knowing and holding to the concept
that the Christ, Truth pursues, overtakes, and
destroys error, and that all things are possible
to God. When we strive to embody and
express Christliness, we are actively glorifying
God and proving His truth.
Life harmonious includes no sense of pain,
worry, lack, victimization, failure, abuse or
being deceived. It is the Creator, Sustainer, and
Maintainer of all being and acts to keep us
healthy, mobile, strong, and well. This life that
is God is all-harmonious in every way, and
never one iota less. We are not a partial
beneficiary of life, but a full expression of it,

with no weak spots or missing attributes.
"Spiritual perception brings out the
possibilities of being, destroys reliance on
aught but God, and so makes man the image
of his Maker in deed and in truth.
God is at once the center and circumference
of being." (Science & Health 203: 13, 32-1)

Isaiah 26:3

Thou will keep him in perfect peace, whose
mind is stayed on thee.

Everything is as real as you make it, and no
more so. What you see, hear feel, is a mode
of consciousness, and can have no other
reality than the sense you entertain of it.
Matter is a subjective state of mortal mind, a
thought projected. If then the human body is
a subjective state of consciousness, or a
projection of thought, then the control of the
body begins with the control of our thoughts.
But its divine Truth not positive thinking that
makes things right. We need to put the
illusive concepts of the human mind- its false
fearful mortal thoughts aside and let the
beauty and wholeness of the divine Mind,
God, be revealed in and through us. This Mind
is a mind of goodness, peace, joy, wisdom,
patience, forgiveness, and health. Also a mind
of Love.

He restoreth my soul

True peace is a quality of divinity which holds men in in perfect harmony, immune to evil suggestions. It provides limitless opportunities of selfless service and collective security. Experience shows that those who believe evil is a power are wrong. When crime is met courageously, it loses its baldness, "Resist the devil, and he will flee from you" "Fret not thyself because of evil doers **Psalm 37**. Also Jesus promised to leave us peace that no man can take away from you. "The great truth in the science of being, that the real man was, is, and ever shall be perfect, is incontrovertible; for if man is the image, reflection of God, he is neither inverted nor subverted, but upright and Godlike". (Science & health 200:16)

This is the truth about man and yet events in our human experience, the media and many active agencies try to convince us the false is the truth about man. That instead of being God's idea, he apparently lacks much which he needs to work at, find or accomplish to make him happy.

Here man should refuse to be mesmerised by all this negativity or unbearable symptoms, and resolutely work mentally to prove the unreality of the whole evil transaction. It matters not what seems to be happening as the spiritual fact about it, is never displaced. The idea is the exact reverse of the situation, and being ever present, it is instantly available. Its action cannot be obstructed delayed, or rendered ineffective, for it is a divinely constituted presence. One needs not to " make" it do anything but let it unfold in God's own way and time. God is attending to

His universe all the time, there is uninterrupted continuity of governing by God which might not be so obvious to us. Refuse to give this false picture audience, always remember error has no mouthpiece or audience. In this world-mesmerism of clashing wills and conflicting human opinions let us never mistake the false for the eternal. Another great fact is that human opinions come to naught or no effect.

God's kingdom is come. It is here and now. But in demonstrating this, let us remember that if one would really bring peace to the world, he must first of all be at peace with himself, his family, his friends, his neighbours, work mates and business associates.

Rejoice always! It is a mistake to confine joy to circumstances or things. He who can rejoice even when things go wrong is one for whom things will soon go right. Light and joy go hand in hand, as do darkness and sorrow; but as light dispels darkness, so does joy dissolve sorrow. The two cannot exist in the same place at the same time. There are no tears in heaven. Do not concern yourself about anything but rejoice that wonderful things are going on.

Joy is not merely an effect: it is also cause. It is not only a result of harmonious conditions, it produces them. It is a restorer. Joy is the outcome of faith. True joy comes with walking with God- let your joy be that "You are a beloved child of God".

We embrace our world within ourselves. All that exists as persons, places and things lives only within our own consciousness. We could never become aware of anything outside the realm of our own mind. And all that is within is our mental kingdom which is joyously and harmoniously directed and sustained by the laws of

Christ/Truth. We do not direct or enforce these laws; they eternally operate within us, and govern the world without.

The peace within becomes the harmony without. As our thought takes on the nature of this inner freedom, it loses its sense of fear, doubt, or discouragement. As the realisation of our dominion dawns in thought, more assurance, confidence, and certainty become evident. We become a new being, and the world reflects back to us our own higher attitude toward it. Gradually our understanding of our fellow man as "all in one eternal being", unfolds to us from within, and more love flows out from us, more tolerance, cooperativeness, helpfulness and compassion, and we find the world responds to our newer concept of it, and then all the universe rushes to us to pour its riches and treasures in our lap.

Isaiah 43: 2

When you passest through the waters, I will be with you; and through the rivers, they shall not overflow you. When thou walkest through the fire, thou shall not be burned, neither shall the flame kindle upon thee.

Romans 8: 28, 31

28-And we know that all things work together for good to them that love God,..

31- What shall we say to these things? If God be for us who can be against us?

Jeremiah 29:11

For I know the thoughts that I think toward you, saith the Lord, thoughts of peace, and not of evil, to give you an expected end.

Expect good from unexpected places. Though we might have lost everything in the way of material possessions, our spiritual wholeness and dominion are intact and will forever remain so. We are eternally maintained and sustained by Spirit not matter. We are already spiritually whole, complete, pure, innocent and safe. We need to see devastation not as a fixed fact, but as a material picture that must be rejected.

He leadeth me in the paths of righteousness for His name's sake

Spirit is the only creator, and man including the universe is His spiritual concept. We learn that moment by moment, God's provision for His own expression is supporting our entire experience. When we understand that the source and substance of all-being is Spirit, not matter, we stop believing that any external, material cause can affect our lives in any way. Let's celebrate that, God's intelligence, understanding and wisdom is infinite and beyond measure, and understanding that man is inseparable from this intelligence, wisdom and understanding is awesome. Leaning on God's infinite ability to take care of us, we are sustained and cared for, no matter what the circumstances seem to be.

In these strenuous times, the full weight of spiritual thinking must be called upon to meet evil at its source, to meet it as the wicked perversion of everything good. To be safe, we must listen, and know forcefully; each day that God, good, is everywhere, and that He governs and controls our thinking, and that no other control can exist or operate.
Every true thought that man has, comes from

God, and anything unlike God, whether it is illness, lack or war, can be proved to be unreal and powerless, since they have no place in this universe.

He leadeth me in the paths of righteousness for his name's sake

How to demonstrate the truth: in John 12:32 Jesus said if I be lifted up from the earth, I will draw all man unto me. This means there is no separation between you and everybody else. The "I" means everyone's identity. The truth about you is the truth about everybody else whether they know it or not. The "I" of me is also the "I" of everyone and everything including a blade of grass, tree, flower or animal.

Things we see with our eyes or hear with our ears are lies about God's creation.

Right where we see an ugly old man, sick, selfish person; right there is the beautiful flawless innocent, spotless, unblemished lamb of God. God's child is healthy, happy, peaceful, kind, pure, intelligent, comforted, perfect and wholly spiritual. He is tender, loving, loved, loveable despite everything to the contrary.

" A human being is part of a whole, called by us – universe, - a part limited in time and space. He experiences himself, his thoughts and feelings as something separated from the rest... a kind of prison for us, restricting us to our personal desires and to affection for a few persons nearest to us. Our task must be to free ourselves from this prison by widening our circle of compassion to embrace all living creatures and the whole of nature in its beauty." Quote Albeit Einstein

We need not fear or accept any report that stems from the belief that we are on our own and exposed to various harmful illusions. God supplies us with the inspiration we need, He never asks us to do anything which is impossible. Christ/ Truth is our healer.

The Christ is never fearful, discouraged, or uninspired nor is the victim of world mesmerism. The Christ is your identity, it is you as God knows you, it is you as you really are! You cannot heal whilst you see yourself as a mere mortal or whilst you still see others in the same way.

Proverbs 1: 10, 20, 33

10- If sinners entice thee, consent thou not

20-wisdom crieth out; she uttereth her voice
in the streets.

33- whoso hearkeneth unto me shall dwell
safely and shall be quiet from fear of evil.

James 3: 17, 18

17-The wisdom that is from above is first pure,
then peaceable, gentle, and easy to be
entreated, full of mercy and good fruits,
without partiality, and without hypocrisy. 18-
And the fruit of righteousness is sown in peace
of them that make peace.

Isaiah 45: 12

I have made the earth, and created man upon
it; I, even my hands, have stretched out the
heavens, and all their host have I commanded.
I have raised him up in righteousness, and I
will direct all his ways:

Psalms 33: 4, 5

4- For the word of the Lord is right; and all his works are done in truth.

5- He loveth righteousness and judgement: the earth is full of the goodness of the Lord.

As our Master Jesus said that the kingdom of heaven is at hand, then God and heaven are here and now; and a change in human consciousness, from sin to holiness, would reveal this wonder of being.

Life is deathless, it is the origin and ultimate of man, never attainable through death, but gained by walking in the pathway of Truth.

Yea, though I walk through the valley of the shadow of death, I will fear no evil;...

" To ignore God as of little use in sickness is a mistake. Instead of thrusting Him aside in times of trouble and waiting for the hour of strength in which to acknowledge.
Him, we should learn that He can do all things for us in sickness as in health". (Science & Health 166: 16)

Evil is a lie, also called animal magnetism or aggressive mental suggestion. It is nothing, no thing. It has no father, no mother, no source of origin. It has no law to operate under, nor any substance to manipulate.

As a logical conclusion we can know that evil, having no source or cause, can have no effect, no result; no planned action; no substance for expression, no evidence, no reality. As long as we do not mentally challenge error's aggressiveness with spiritual weapons, we will remain victims of evil. We must refute every suggestion at the door of our thought before it convinces us and takes control. Remember error is the shadow of death, only the shadow therefore not reality! God did not make it and God made all that was made.

Always we look at the Allness of God and not focus on the problem. The more we focus on the problem the more we magnify it, and this way, we are belittling God. If we find ourselves beset by fear, stop and remember that God is not the author of confusion, but of peace, that from Him comes every perfect gift.

God is no respecter of persons, that is; what He is to one, He is to all. It is His good pleasure to bestow the kingdom of universal and eternal harmony upon all His children.

As we hold to these truths and turn a deaf ear to all the arguments of error, fear will decrease. And one fear overcome makes possible the overcoming of others. We should be calm, and endeavor to listen to what God is telling us from within.

It is the lie which says we are not good enough or do not have the right understanding. We need to discipline our thought about everything and everyone that our thought rests upon. Every person we see and know is part of our spiritual body and we need to see them correctly. If we are resentful of ourselves or anybody - that is injurious to ourselves. Remember perfect God, perfect man and perfect universe. I always remind myself that "I AM THAT I AM" not "this I am". This way I am identifying myself with the CHRIST. God is expressing Himself as me. "Reality is spiritual, harmonious, immutable, immortal, divine, eternal. Nothing unspiritual can be real, harmonious, or eternal. Sin, sickness and mortality are the suppositional antipodes of spirit, and must be contradictions of reality". (Science & Health 335: 27)

Philippians 4: 8, 9

8- whatsoever things are true, whatsoever things are honest, whatsoever things are just, whatsoever things are pure, whatsoever things are lovely, whatsoever things are of good report; if there be any virtue, and if there be any praise, think on these things. 9- and the God of peace shall be with you.

Psalms 33: 10, 11

10- The lord bringeth the counsel of the heathen to naught: he maketh the devices of the people of non-`effect. 11 The counsel of the lord standeth forever, the thoughts of his heart to all generations.

" If we concede the same reality to discord as to harmony, discord has as lasting a claim upon us as harmony". (Science & Health 186: 22-24)

"We must learn that evil is the awful deception and unreality of existence. Evil is not supreme; good is not helpless; nor are the so-called laws of matter primary, and the law of Spirit secondary" (Science & Health 207: 9-13).

This is a great Hymn in Christian Science:
Hymn 10

1- All power is given unto our Lord, On Him we place reliance: With truth from His sacred word We bid our foes defiance. With Him we shall prevail, What ever shall assail; He is our shield and tower, Almighty is His power; His Kingdom is forever.

2- Rejoice ye people, praise His name, His care doth e'er surround us. His love to error's thraldom came, And from its chains unbound us. Our Lord is God alone, No other power we own; No other voice we heed, No other help we need; His kingdom is forever.

3- O then give thanks to God on high, Who life to all is giving; The hosts of death before Him fy, In Him we all are living. Then let us know no fear, Our King is ever near; Our stay and fortress strong, Our strength, our hope, our song; His kingdom is forever.

Thou preparest a table before me in the presence of my enemies; thou annointest my head with oil; my cup runneth over

God has infinite resources with which to bless mankind. Always be aware of the boundless opportunities and abundance of all good that God gives to his children without measure. We put ceilings and limits ourselves to what we can receive or achieve. Gratitude and joy are essential to receiving from our God.

I pray to know that "the I am that I see" and that everyone sees is not me at all. For only God knows who I really am and the truth about me. I have never left heaven for earth. I live in the atmosphere of God's divine love in eternal life. I am the expression of who God is and God is expressing Himself as me. And it is God doing the expressing not me. No evil suggestions can impress me, fool me, confuse me, frighten, and make me believe lies about myself or anyone else. They also cannot believe lies about me as my Mind is their Mind, because God is the only Mind.

This Mind is always peaceful, understood, calm, serene, loving, intelligent, all-knowing, all-wise and restful. It is always inspired, hopeful, joyful and contented. Always claim the power of the word you are reading. Do not believe in a personal problem for there is none, there is only one "I" and He is God, nothing can touch Him and therefore nothing can touch you! ". Hate no one; for hatred is a plaque-spot that spreads its virus and kills at last" (M.B.E miscellaneous writings 1883-1886)

" We should measure our love for God by our love for man..." (M.B.E miscellaneous writings 1883- 1886)

Isaiah 25:1

O Lord, thou art my God; I will exalt thee, I will praise thy name; for thou hast done wonderful things; thy counsels of old are faithfulness and truth.

Opportunity is where God is; thus, never past, never separate from Him, and never out of grasp. Always present, constantly renewed, ever available, the opportunity to be well, happy, and good awaits our recognition and utilisation. As we dwell increasingly in the consciousness of God's omnipotence, evil is seen as a dream and good as the permanent fact. Then the future is faced with confidence, and thought is lifted into scientific realisation of the eternal actualities of being.

We must ever remember that God is Love, ever -present, ever-available, and ever- able to destroy every evil that would assail mortal man. A little love realised will ameliorate any condition, situation, or circumstance that is coloured with fear, hate in our home relations, politics, business, or social life.

Evil pretends to have power, tenacity, and continuity. But these are qualities of

Truth, not error; of good not evil. Real health is tenacious, prosperity is persistent, progress is perpetual, for good alone endures. Knowing that God, Principle, is the only law giver, we see that error is without law, thus without power of enforcement, intelligence to develop, or ability to persist. This is a helpful thing to know in any phase of evil. With JOY and FEARLESSNESS let us realise that evil which actually has no being today, cannot be real and progressing tomorrow. Thus we can deny every phase of error and its every claim of development and perpetuity.

Surely goodness and mercy shall follow me all the days of my life,...

Always continue to claim the power of the word of God you are reading and declaring, for it is not only word, but also God with us. The truth of perfect God, perfect man and perfect universe is so wonderful and inspiring and evident when demonstrated. The Christ in man is always obedient and always receptive. The Christ is man's true and only selfhood. The kingdom of heaven is within you.
Demonstrate your kingdom of heaven and make it realisable!

Let's make a resolution to wake up every morning and see perfection, a perfect cause and perfect effect, perfect God and perfect man, refuse to make any kind of exception, refuse to admit the slightest imperfection in ourselves, our friends, in our so-called enemies, in our affairs and in the affairs of the world.

Take a radical stand for the perfection of God, everything and everybody He has made; look upon the world with God's eyes and see it as He sees it and refuse to see it any other way. See the perfection of God, Man and the universe. "Success, prosperity and happiness follow the footsteps of unselfed motives" (M.B.E. Collection)

Romans 8: 35, 38, 39 39-

35- Who shall separate us from the love of Christ?

38- For I am persuaded, that neither death, nor life, nor angels, nor principalities, nor powers, nor things present, nor things to come,

39- Nor height, nor depth, nor any other creature, shall be able to separate us from the love of God, which is in Christ Jesus our Lord.

"Success in life depends upon persistent effort, upon the improvement of moments more than upon any other one thing. A great amount of time is consumed in talking nothing, doing nothing, and indecision as to what one should do. If one would be successful in the future, let him make the most of the present". (M.B.E miscellaneous writings 1883-1886) "Rushing around smartly is no proof of accomplishing much". (M.B.E. miscellaneous writings 1883-1886) "There is no excellency without labour, and the time to work is now. Only by persistent, unremitting, straightforward toil; by turning neither to the right nor to the left, seeking no other pursuit or pleasure than that which cometh from God, can you win and wear the crown of the faithful". (M.B.E. miscellaneous writings 1883-1886)

1 Peter 3:13

And who is he that can harm you, if ye be
followers of that which is good?

111 John 1: 2, 4, 11

11- Beloved, follow not that which is evil, but that which is good. He that doeth good is of God

2- Beloved, I wish above all things that thou mayest prosper and be in health, even as thy soul prospereth.

4- I have no greater joy than to hear that my children walk in truth.

" The understanding that Life is god, Spirit, lengthens our days by strengthening our trust in the deathless reality of Life, its almightiness and immortality" (Science & Health 48:27)

Life is substance, original, self-existent, self sustaining. So understood Life is God,

Spirit, the divine Principle of all existence. Life is not dependent on something other than itself for existence or a medium external to itself and unlike itself for expression.

Life expresses itself in living. Its expression is in individual spiritual identities, in spiritual man and spiritual universe. That the universe exists in Life is more accurate than that Life exists in the universe.

There is a law of God that is applicable to every conceivable phase of human experience, and no situation or condition can present itself to mortal thought which can possibly exist outside the direct influence of this infinite law. The effect of the operation of law is always to correct, and govern, to harmonise and adjust.

Whatever is out of order or discordant can have no basic principle of its own, but must come under the direct government of God through what may be termed God's law of adjustment. We are not responsible for the carrying out of this law; Mind is already at work. Let's stay clear of fear and put out of thought that Mind does not know our plight, or that wisdom lacks the intelligence necessary to bring about rescue.

Asking God to be God is a vain repetition. God has no need of being adjusted. The only place where there is need of adjustment is the human consciousness. But unless human consciousness appeals to the divine law, unless it is willing to lay down its own sense of human will, and stop human planning, put aside human pride, ambition, and vanity, there is no room for the law of adjustment to operate.

Conclusion

Since Mind is one infinite, self-conscious Being, then everything in the universe exists because this Mind has unfolded itself, out into all existing things, out into infinity.

One infinite eternal Mind precludes the possibility of lesser mind. Therefore, so-called mortal mind is never an entity or a mind, but that which has no existence and does not fill space. It is ignorance or a false sense of the allness of God.

When we sense things which are not taking place at all, this is false belief or false sense. Such is all mental malpractice. Mental malpractice is something that we sense but is not going on at all. (e.g.) moving on a train that is still standing).

Please bear in mind that the one infinite consciousness is everybody's consciousness. We do not have a consciousness of our own, any more than an individual ray of light has its own light. The light of the sun is the light of every individual ray. Just so, Truth, being universal consciousness, is the consciousness of every individual.

But malpractice claims to be a universal consciousness with everything in a sense of reversion. It claims that the universal false sense consciousness is the consciousness of every individual man and woman. This false sense is what we are to uncover as nothing and nobody!

Conception of mal-practice (personal); we should understand that mental malpractice is false sense only, and not something that we are experiencing.

Usually, we believe a person is thinking??? about another person, thereby harming that person through this mental process.

But mental malpractice is entirely impersonal. A person has nothing to do with this false sense, and to be effectually dealt with, it must be understood that not actually recognising a false sense for what it is, is to be in danger of believing it. We should know evil aright and reduce its claim to its proper denominator, NOBODY! NOTHING! And then we are its Master not servant! "... to understand God is the work of eternity, and demands absolute consecration of thought, energy and desire". (Science & Health 3:16)

Printed in Great Britain
by Amazon

67054052R00068